Praise for Kayleen Reusser's books:

We Fought to Win: American World War II Veterans Share Their Stories (Book 1, World War II Legacies)

"This book is highly recommended as it importantly documents the experiences and sacrifices of these remarkable Hoosier veterans who are a part of The Greatest Generation." Christopher Wiljer, librarian

"Reusser has served us well to talk with veterans from her region to preserve their stories for posterity while there is still time." Shirley Brosius, author of Sisterhood of Faith.

**

They Did It for Honor: Stories of American WWII Veterans (Book 2, World War II Legacies)

"The information shared here, from the hearts of 34 World War Two Veterans, is simply stunning. Being a 'veteran' myself (Vietnam), and a long-time appreciator of the 'service to mankind' concept, this book really got my attention." Curtis Rose, sculptor

"Reusser's efforts are keeping alive a valuable piece of history." Debbie Wilson, author of Tiger in the Shadows

"The variety of male and female veterans' stories from all branches of the military during WWII was an interesting and historical account from their perspectives." Barb Smith, military family member

**

We Gave Our Best: American WWII Veterans Tell Their Stories (Book 3, World War II Legacies)

"Each interview includes the veteran's before-during-and-after narrative: What each did prior to the war, their recollections of military service during the war, and how their lives unfolded after the war." Carolyn Kramer, teacher

"Their stories are written in short, easy-to-read biographies and are eye-witness accounts ranging from their wartime experiences to heartwarming memories. The stories are enhanced by photos and timely explanations of WWII history." Shana Neuenschwander, librarian

D-Day:
Soldiers, Sailors and Airmen Tell about Normandy

World War II Insider Series
Book 1

Kayleen Reusser

Kayleen Reusser Media

D-Day: Soldiers, Sailors and Airmen Tell about Normandy
First published in the United States by Kayleen Reusser Media.

Printed in the United States.

KayleenReusser.com

ISBN 978-1-7325172-2-6

Cover illustration by Kayleen Reusser

Printed in the United States of America

The information provided within this book is for general informational purposes only. While the author has tried to provide correct information, there are no representations or warranties, express or implied, about the completeness, accuracy, reliability, suitability or availability with respect to the information, products, services, or related graphics contained in this book for any purpose. Any use of this information is at one's own risk.

Photographs throughout the book are courtesy of veterans, National Archives and the author.

Acknowledgments

This book is a sincere thanks to the veterans mentioned in this book: Bob Batchelder, George Banky, Gene Cogan, Gene Dettmer, Charles Dunwoody, Al Edwards, Dr. Jim Fall, Harrison Hull, Don Lee, Don LeMaster, Dean Reckard, Leo Scheer, Bob Staggs, Gene Valentine, Richard Willey, Ray Willig, Don Wolfe. Without their courage and dedication, I don't know where we would be today.

Credit goes to people who assisted me in my efforts to create this book – Beth Steury who helped with layout and the Wells County Public Library (Indiana) staff which provided visual and other help. Families of the veterans often aided in arranging interviews and providing information about loved ones.

Thanks to my parents, Forace Hale and Evelyn Joan Brewer. I used to tease Dad for the hours he spent watching documentaries about World War II. Now I think he'd be proud of my efforts to bring to life the stories of the men and women who served there. Mom was a teacher so I grew up with a love for books, words, and reading. It's due to her early encouragement that my goal of being an author has been accomplished.

A special thanks to my husband, John, a retired Air Force airman. Without his enthusiasm for serving his country and willingness to preserve our country's military heritage, I would find it difficult to continue with this project. He has often accompanied me to interviews and lent much assistance, especially with aviation questions. Of course, he considers it pretty sweet to have a wife who couldn't wait to take part in a World War II tour of Europe. Love, always.

Introduction

World War II was a monumental event in the lives of most people who lived during the years of 1939-1945. Today it is hard for us to imagine those challenging years when a specter of gloom seemed to creep unrelenting across the world. At times it was not clear how the Allied powers could prevent the Axis Powers -- Germany, Italy, and Japan -- from invading other countries. At one point Great Britain was the only Allied country in Europe to remain unconquered by Germany.

The Allied invasion of Europe at Normandy, which came to be known as D-Day, combined intelligence, creative innovation, overwhelming numbers of troops and weapons, deceptions, international cooperation and committed leadership. It also required great bravery and sacrifice on the part of men who made up D-Day's landing force. Truly, June 6, 1944, was a date for the whole world to remember.

This first book in my World War II Insider series focuses on the courageous acts carried out on June 6, 1944, and the days following to liberate Europe. Of the 150,000+ men who fought at Operation Overlord (code name for the invasion), few are still alive to tell us what it was like to be on those shores and climb the bluffs that hid German soldiers. Those who have shared with me what it was like to launch the massive assault by the Allies that turned the tide of war in Europe are among the last first-hand accounts ever to be available.

Future books in the Insider series will cover Battle of the Bulge, Iwo Jima and Okinawa. Hopefully, these stories will inspire a sense of patriotism, humility for what others have done for us, and appreciation for the hard work and dedication it took to win these battles and ultimately, the war. It has been an honor for me to meet each veteran and hear his story.

Thank a veteran today for his/her service. God bless America!

General Dwight D. Eisenhower gives the order of the Day to paratroopers in England just before they board planes to participate in the first assault in the invasion of Normandy.

In February 1944 General Dwight D. Eisenhower drafted an Order of the Day for June 6, 1944, to be distributed to the Allied expeditionary force on the eve of the D-Day invasion:

"Soldiers, sailors and airmen of the Allied Expeditionary Force!

You are about to embark upon the Great Crusade toward which we have striven these many months. The eyes of the world are upon you. The hopes and prayers of liberty-loving people everywhere march with you.

In company with our brave Allies and brothers-in-arms on other Fronts, you will bring about the destruction of the German war machine, the elimination of Nazi tyranny over the oppressed peoples of Europe and security for ourselves in a free world. Your task will not be an easy one. Your enemy is well trained, well-equipped and battle-hardened. He will fight savagely.

But this is the year 1944! Much has happened since the Nazi triumphs of the 1940-41. The United Nations have inflicted upon the Germans great defeats in open battle, man-to-man.

Our air offensive has seriously reduced their strength in the air and their capacity to wage war on the ground. Our Home Fronts have given us an overwhelming superiority in weapons and munitions of war and placed at our disposal great reserves of trained fighting men. The tide has turned!

The free men of the world are marching together to Victory!

I have full confidence in your courage, devotion to duty and skill in battle. We will accept nothing less than a full victory!

Good luck! And let us all beseech the blessing of Almighty God upon this great and noble undertaking."

**

On June 5, Eisenhower scribbled another note, accepting responsibility for the decision to launch the invasion and full blame should the effort to create a beachhead on the Normandy coast fail. It was never released.

Contents

CHAPTER 1

Preparations for D-Day

American soldiers leave the ramp of a boat after landing on the coast of France under heavy Nazi machine gun fire .

In 1933, Adolph Hitler was appointed Chancellor of Germany. He quickly established a government called the National Socialist German Workers' Party ('Nazis'), which supported his belief in Germany's right to rule the world. During the next several years, the Nazis imprisoned and murdered thousands of people, most notably Jews, whom they deemed destroyers of Germany's culture and economy. By September 1939, Hitler and the Nazis had built up enough military force to quickly and efficiently invade its neighboring country of Poland.

The modern-day village of St. Mere Eglise offers shops and an Old-World charm that attracts tourists.

The siege of the Nazis continued so that by 1940 the country of France was under German rule. For hundreds of years places like the French village of St. Mere Eglise had been filled with farms, cows, and flowers and people who liked to shop, chat and attend church. But when the German military took over, villagers lived in fear of their enemy's guns and authority. Soon, much of the European continent -- Belgium, Yugoslavia, Denmark, Greece, Luxembourg, the Netherlands and Norway – had fallen to Hitler and feared his control.

The dictator of Italy, Benito Mussolini, joined Hitler, as did Hirohito, the Emperor of Japan. Hirohito desired to overtake the people of the Philippines, Singapore, and China and terrorized that part of the world. Together, they formed the Axis powers.

In 1940 Hitler began an aggressive attempt to force yet another country -- England -- into surrendering. For nearly two months German planes dropped bombs on London and other British cities. The people of England lost homes, businesses and lives. Yet, they refused to surrender and won significant battles against Hitler, mostly by air. By 1941, unable to claim victory in England, Hitler turned his focus to overthrowing the Russian government, resulting in the deaths of hundreds of thousands of people.

Americans read with mixed reactions about the massacres happening around the world. While many felt sorry for people suffering under dictators, they were reluctant to get involved, preferring to remain isolated from the world's problems. Their concern was rebuilding America following the horrible economic depression of the 1930s.

Then, on the morning of December 7, 1941, their perspective changed when Japanese planes bombed American naval forces at Pearl Harbor at Hawaii. Every American battleship stationed there—USS *Arizona,* USS *Utah,* USS *Oklahoma,* USS *California,* USS *Nevada,* USS *West Virginia,* USS *Maryland,* USS *Pennsylvania,* USS *Tennessee* — incurred substantial destruction. All but the *Arizona* and *Utah* were later salvaged and repaired. Sadly, 2,403 sailors, soldiers and civilians lost their lives with another 1,000 civilians sustaining injuries.

The USS *Arizona* burns after the Japanese attack on Pearl Harbor on December 7, 1941.

When Americans on the mainland heard about the attack, they were incensed, though most didn't know where Pearl Harbor was. They presented a united front when on December 8 the American Congress declared war on Japan.

American President Franklin D. Roosevelt joined Allied leaders Joseph Stalin of the Soviet Union and Prime Minister of England Winston Churchill in trying to stop the terror and madness of the Axis powers. They called themselves the Allies.

Two long years passed. Resources in the Axis and Allied countries, such as gas, food, clothing, and building materials, stretched thin. People everywhere wondered how much longer the war could continue.

In 1943 General Dwight D. Eisenhower is appointed Supreme Allied Commander of the European Theater of Operations. He will make all decisions regarding D-Day.

In 1943, the Allies began plans for a secret invasion of Europe. American General Dwight D. Eisenhower was appointed Commander of the Supreme Headquarters Allied Expeditionary Force. He and his group of leaders assigned the code name of *Operation Overlord* to the invasion which they hoped would bring an end to the war.

Eisenhower and his leadership team spent much time deciding where the invasion would take place. The English Channel between England and France was narrow near Pas de Calais. But France's wide beaches along a 50-mile strip in the Normandy area offered more strategic opportunities for beach landings. That became the chosen spot.

Spies who worked for the Allies spread the word that an invasion would occur near Pas de Calais. Upon hearing the rumors, Hitler felt well prepared. Over the years, he had planted millions of mines, barriers and gun emplacements along 1,670 miles of the western European coast. He was certain his 'Atlantic Wall', as he called it, would deter the enemy.

Every effort was made to keep the planning of Operation Overlord top-secret. No one wanted Hitler to discover plans were being made to stop his domination of Europe and other parts of the world.

The Allies divided Normandy into five sections. Each one was given a code name. American military forces were in charge of the westernmost beaches they called Utah and Omaha. British troops would land at Gold Beach and the easternmost beach called Sword. The Canadians were assigned Juno Beach.

One major detail had yet to be decided for '*D-Day*' (the nickname given to the invasion) – when would it take place?

Based on weather, moon and tides, Eisenhower selected June 5, 1944.

However, as with most well-laid plans, a last-minute glitch occurred, one that threatened the success of the entire operation.

American President Franklin D. Roosevelt signs the Declaration of War against Japan, December 8, 1941.

CHAPTER 2

—————————— ∽∾∾∽ ——————————

Fighting on the Ground

On the evening of June 4, 156,000 troops cast off from England into the English Channel. Private First Class Richard Willey from Bluffton, Ind., was assigned to the 953rd Army Field Artillery Battalion of the V Corps. Willey had been one of two million American servicemen who sailed from the U.S. in spring 1944 to prepare for the invasion. Many would remain in England until needed in Europe as replacement troops.

In Scotland Willey's unit had trained to shoot 155-millimeter Howitzers on the moors. "We were never told what we were being trained for," said Willey, a Purdue University graduate. "We just figured there would be an invasion somewhere."

As the troops disembarked from England, they were accompanied by ships loaded with 20,000 military vehicles and artillery. The invasion had begun.

American troops brandish their nation's flag as they exit landing crafts to rush the beaches of Normandy.

As the ships quietly traversed the 100-mile stretch towards France, heavy fog and low clouds threatened visibility. Reluctantly, General Eisenhower delayed the invasion for 24 hours. He and his advisors hoped the Nazis would not detect the vast armada sitting in the Channel during the night.

In the pre-dawn hours of June 6, 1944, men of the 467th battalion of the U.S. Army dropped from their boat into the water close to the Normandy shore.

As the ramp of their landing craft drops, soldiers run to shore, hoping to avoid mines and gunfire, guns held high overhead.

The job of the 467th and other companies was to storm Omaha Beach and overtake the Germans. Once the beach was secure, Allied soldiers would rapidly advance inland, destroying enemy resistance.

Landing chin-high, the soldiers spread out, guns held above their heads as they waded through the freezing waters of the English Channel to shore.

It was not an easy journey. As the Allies staggered onto Omaha Beach, they dodged mines, machine-gun fire and barbed wire. Those that made it across the roughly 400 yards of beach then had to climb the brambled incline of the bluffs where the enemy was hidden.

"We tried to run up the hill, but their 88s stopped us," said Private First Class Bob Staggs. Although initially surprised by the invasion, German crews with big guns overlooking the shore began firing on the troops and ships with unerring accuracy.

The German cannons with shells measuring 88 millimeters in diameter were designed primarily as antiaircraft artillery weapons, but worked effectively on ground troops. From their armed strongpoint behind heavily-fortified pillboxes the German soldiers had a sweeping view of the beachhead and Americans landing there.

Staggs, a native of Selma, Ind., and the rest of his unit had trained for weeks in southwest England for the amphibious invasion. Drafted into the U.S. Army in 1943, Staggs completed boot camp at Fort Eustis, Virginia, before leaving with his unit on a troop ship for Exmouth.

When troops of the 467th had received orders to modify the half-tracks (armored personnel vehicles), scuttlebutt ran rampant. "We put exhaust pipes in the air and covered spark plugs with clay," said Staggs. "That made the half-tracks waterproof. We guessed we may be preparing for a battle over water."

Donald Lee of Auburn, Ind., was a newlywed when he fought with an antiaircraft / artillery unit at Omaha Beach. Lee had married his girlfriend, Lucille, during a three-day pass in October 1943. Thoughts of love and romance were far from Lee's mind as he viewed with horror the tragic scenes around him after the firing began. "Dead bodies of American soldiers floated on the water," he said. "On shore they were stacked like cordwood."

The battle at Omaha Beach lasted all day and all night. On D-Day+1, Don LeMaster of Ossian, Ind., arrived to see Sherman tanks sunk in the water near the shore.

LeMaster was assigned to a quartermaster unit that maintained Army trucks and obtained supplies for troops. "They must have driven off of the LSTs (landing, ship, tank vessels) into too deep of water," he said. "Their four-man crews didn't have a chance of surviving."

Don LeMaster

As LeMaster and other troops made it to shore, they ducked behind hedgerows which served as barricades. "When a shell came at us, it lifted us off of the ground," he added.

Ray Willig

By the time Ray Willig arrived at Omaha on D-Day+4 (June 10) with the 30th Infantry Division-Artillery, the area resembled mass chaos. "Small arms fire was non-stop," he said.

Willig, born in 1926 in Fort Wayne, Ind., had lied about his age to enlist in the Army in 1943. "I said I was 17 years old when I was 16," he said. "Friends were serving and I wanted to as well."

At Liverpool, England, Willig bivouacked with soldiers in a forest for several weeks while learning to shoot 105-millimeter shells and other battle maneuvers.

At Utah Beach Eugene Dettmer of Fort Wayne saw men get blown up. Although Allied casualties at Utah numbered fewer (300) than those on nearby Omaha Beach (5,000), still the drama was before each man.

Attached to the Third Army with 468th AAA Battery C, Dettmer had been drafted during his senior year of Ossian High School. After completing basic training at Fort Eustis, Virginia, Dettmer trained at Fort Miles Standish in Taunton, Mass. In March 1944 Dettmer and thousands of other soldiers disembarked by ship from the East Coast of the U.S. for Scotland.

This bunker on Utah Beach captured on June 6, 1944, becomes the U.S. Navy communication center until October 1944.

Continuing on to France, the soldiers could little have imagined their involvement in one of the deadliest battles in the history of the world. "Our landing at Utah Beach was off by a day due to weather," said Dettmer. "That may have confused the Germans, but they still put up a good fight."

On D-Day, the quarter-mile stretch of sand on Omaha Beach to the cliffs where Germans fired is covered with mines, barbed wire and other obstacles that threaten the lives of Allied soldiers.

CHAPTER 3

Charles Burns Dunwoody – Army Chaplain

During the war, many soldiers turned to the church for spiritual and emotional support. Nearly 8,000 clergy enrolled as chaplains in the military. Churches provided Bibles and devotional literature for the troops.

Chaplain's Assistant Charles Dunwoody is wounded at D-Day and later is given a Purple Heart for sustaining injuries during battle.

At Normandy Charles B. Dunwoody served as a chaplain's assistant for the 83rd Division of the U.S. Army.

Born in 1917 on a farm in Darke County in Ohio, Dunwoody graduated from Versailles High School in 1935, an accomplishment somewhat unusual during the Depression when many young men quit school to work.

Dunwoody farmed until October 1943 when he was drafted into the Army. After completing basic training at Camp Atterbury in Indiana, Dunwoody was assigned to the infantry with the 83rd Division and trained for battle with the Tennessee Maneuvers.

Dunwoody had attended church regularly with his family. When his rifle unit's chaplain lost an assistant, the chaplain asked Dunwoody's company commander to allow Dunwoody to take the assistant's place. The commander didn't want to let Dunwoody go. "After hunting squirrels and rabbits on the farm, I could shoot well and he thought I would be valuable to him," said Dunwoody. Still, the request was granted and Dunwoody was transferred to work with the chaplain, a minister from Florida.

Dunwoody contributed to the services by playing a portable musical instrument called a 'suitcase organ'. "We carried it on a trailer behind a jeep," he said. "It had a keyboard and pedals that we used to play hymns. We followed the troops and set up wherever we could." Dunwoody's musical experience consisted of taking a few lessons as a child from his mother.

In between military conflicts, Dunwoody and other chaplains offer hope and encouragement to weary troops by leading in music, prayer and preaching.

At Omaha Beach, the chaplains delayed services until the fighting had subsided. Despite being a good shot, Dunwoody was injured and spent several weeks in a hospital. He later was awarded a Purple Heart.

Chaplains preached and led singing wherever troops with war-torn nerves were bivouacked. "In France we held services in villages so residents could attend," he said. On one occasion the chaplains gave coal to two elderly villagers who had run out.

Chaplains represented all faiths, including Catholic, Protestants and Jewish "We chaplains didn't criticize other churches," said Dunwoody. "We worked together."

After the war, the congregation of the church at St. Mere Eglise, a village situated five miles from Omaha Beach, replaces their broken stained glass windows. They choose designs of Allied military figures and those that picture the liberation, including paratroopers in the early hours of June 6, 1944. The windows will forever reflect the villagers' gratefulness for their rescue.

CHAPTER 4

Fighting from the Sea

As Alfred Edwards' rhino barge carried tanks and troops to Omaha Beach, he prepared for the moment the vessel would reach shore. He would then drop the ramp and stand aside for soldiers on board to rush off. Stationed at the back exposed Edwards as a target to German guns on the bluff overlooking the beach. However, Edwards knew this was war and there was no going back.

Moments later, his breakfast threatened to make a sudden reappearance as soldiers, many in their teens, ran from the vessel before suddenly jerking from the impact of bullets ripping through their bodies. He watched in horror as they fell lifeless into the surf and on the beachhead.

The loss of life appalled Edwards. Still, he had been raised to believe in giving one's all for country.

A native of Fort Wayne, Ind., Edwards and his two brothers had listened to their father, Albert Edwards, tell stories of immigrating to America in 1921. "Dad fought in the British army during World War I," said Alfred Edwards. "He taught

American troops on a navy vessel anxiously await the moment when the back ramp will drop, signaling their approach to Omaha Beach.

us to respect this country because America had been good to him."

After being drafted into the Navy in 1943, Al Edwards completed Seabee training at Camp Perry, Virginia. "I was trained to use bulldozers and road equipment," he said. His unit, the 111th Naval Construction Battalion, was shipped to England, while his two brothers also completed military service.

Originally, Al Edwards' Seabee duties for D-Day had been for land, rather than sea. But like many events at Normandy, plans changed and he was re-assigned. The willingness of Edwards and others to adapt on the battlefield would combine to form a united, victorious effort.

During Operation Neptune, as the journey across the Channel was called, more than 4,300 Navy battleships, cruisers and destroyers gave much-needed protection to ground troops. While most of the naval support at D-Day arrived from the American, British and Canadian military divisions, additional assistance was provided by Norway, Holland, Poland, Denmark, Greece.

Massive German concrete gun emplacements situated five miles beyond the shoreline targeted the ships. German spotters close to the beach radioed coordinates of select naval targets to shell back to the gun crews.

This German gun emplacement at Longues-sur-Mer is one of three located five miles behind Omaha Beach.

Gun crews launched volleys at the ships with deadly accuracy. Mines embedded in the sand posed equally dangerous threats to the Allied naval vessels. "They could blow us up as we neared the shore," said Edwards.

Like many replacement troops, Dean Reckard had his first experience in combat at Normandy. As a Machinist Mate 3rd Class aboard the USS *Amesbury* DE 66, Reckard helped in the engine room as the Destroyer escort scouted the English Channel for enemies in the water. "During D-Day, our crew went after two German subs and sunk them," he said.

Growing up on a farm in Whitley County, Ind., in the 1920's, Reckard loved being around water. "I learned to swim in Clear Creek," he said. After graduating from Huntington Township High School, he was drafted in 1943 into the U.S. Navy.

The Amesbury, equipped with a 50-caliber machine gun, 20-millimeter gun and antitank-submarine mortars, sailed beside troop ships as part of a convoy of protection across the Atlantic to Europe. It searched for German submarines across the Atlantic. "Our crew patrolled the waters while escorting troop ships and dropping depth charges on the enemy," he said.

Despite its armor, the crew of 125 men aboard the Amesbury was aware of the ship's vulnerability. "When German bullets bounced on our deck, we knew we were what the enemy was shooting for," he said.

CHAPTER 5

An Unexpected Hero at D-Day -
Andrew Higgins

One man never stepped foot on a Normandy beach, yet was credited by General Dwight D. Eisenhower for helping to win the war.

Andrew Higgins was a New Orleans business owner who made boats for swamps and bayous. When the war began, Higgins studied sketches of watercraft the Japanese used for battle. Higgins adapted a version of a boat for military use, which he then manufactured in great quantities for the Allies.

The self-propelled barges called LCVPs (landing craft, vehicle, personnel) could carry 36 troops. Alongside a troop ship, soldiers would transfer to the Higgins boats via rope ladders. In addition to troops, Higgins boats could carry up to four tons of cargo, including jeeps and trucks.

A Higgins boat required four crewmen, including an engineer who helped it move at 14 miles per hour.

This sculpture at Utah Beach illustrates how a Higgins boat enables troops to make a quick exit onto the beaches.

Close to shore a Higgins boat could empty its contents and make a getaway in as little as three minutes. In situations where defense was necessary two crewmen fired swiveling 30-caliber machine guns.

The Higgins boats, measuring 36 feet, were made of plywood. This could have made them useless against shells bursting from the shore. Andrew Higgins ordered his factory workers to add a quarter-inch steel plate sheathing on the retractable bow. This doubled as a full-width ramp. Soldiers were not only protected by the armored ramp but reinforced sides offered protection as well.

Higgins' 30,000 employees built 20,000 LCVPs (landing, craft, vessel, personnel) during the war. So popular were the boats that they took American troops to shore in every major amphibious assault of World War II, including D-Day, North Africa, Italy, southern France and the Pacific.

When interested personnel began planning a museum honoring D-Day, they chose to build it in downtown New Orleans, due to the significant contributions of Andrew

The World War II Museum in New Orleans houses thousands of items from the war.

Higgins. Today, the museum is renamed The National WWII Museum. Among its collection is a replica of a Higgins boat. The museum is located at Andrew Higgins Drive between Camp and Magazine Streets. Search Nationalww2museum.org for more information.

Posters created throughout the war encourage young men to enlist by going to their nearest recruiting station of the armed service of their choice.

CHAPTER 6

George Banky – 'Sitting Duck'

"I knew what it must be like to be one of those small plastic ducks floating in water used for target practice at a carnival," said George Banky of Waterloo, Iowa. During D-Day, he and a small group of seamen volunteered for an assignment that left them virtually with no protection from the enemy's guns.

Banky was one of 18 sailors who volunteered for a 'special' assignment without knowing details. Afterward, the volunteers discovered the mission was special due to its high-risk factor.

Born in Boston, Mass., in 1926, Banky was 17 years old when he convinced his mother to give her written consent for him to enlist in the Navy. In early 1944, after completing boot camp at San Diego, Banky sailed with thousands of other troops to England. For the next several months they completed long, hikes and learned how to climb in and out of navy ships using rope ladders.

A convoy of ships cross the English Channel for D-Day. Balloons in the air are designed to prevent enemy planes from strafing.

In the weeks leading up to Operation Overlord, Banky heard scuttlebutt (military gossip) about a major invasion. "I wanted to be part of it," he said.

The group would sail a flat-bottomed boat called LCF (landing craft flak) in front of the Normandy beach during battle. The purpose was to create a decoy for the German troops.

To make their position even more dangerous, the LCF was ill-equipped with armament for defense. "All we had were small anti-aircraft weapons," said Banky. "Other seamen thought we were strange to volunteer for such a dangerous job."

Banky may have thought he and his crew were indeed crazy as at D-Day the Germans strafed their small vessel. The LCF crew that had positioned itself to draw fire received some protection by U.S. naval destroyers, cruisers and battleships firing on the enemy.

During the first several hours, it was difficult to tell if the diversionary efforts of the LCF aided American troops. Their attempts to attack German soldiers hidden in the gun emplacements seemed futile. "The Germans were safely dug in, so it was difficult to oust them," said Banky.

Eventually, Allied forces gained ground, advancing on shore while beating the Germans back. Miraculously, none of the LCF's crew was injured.

"It's not fun being fired on in the middle of combat," said Banky. "But that's what war is. You have to get yourself mentally fitted for it."

CHAPTER 7

Fighting in the Air

By early 1944, dozens of Allied air bases had been established in England and British and American air crews increased their number of bombing missions in France and Germany. The Army Air Corps' B-17 Flying Fortresses and B-24 Liberators conducted daytime raids of German military, transportation (trains), and industrial sites, while the Royal Air Force (RAF) bombed German targets at night.

Outside the English village of Muching Green, Donald Wolfe of Fort Wayne flew short bombing missions ('sorties') with his B-26 crew in preparation for D-Day. The B-26 Marauder was powerful with two 2,000-horsepower engines and machine guns and skill was needed to fly them.

Hundreds of crews were lost during training at MacDill Air Force Base, Fla., where Wolfe completed pilot training. A popular saying among pilots and flight crews was, 'One a day in Tampa Bay.'

To relieve the stress, crews assigned macabre nicknames to the B-26s, including 'Widowmaker' and 'Flying Coffin.'

A raid by the American 8th Air Force on an aircraft factory in Germany hits its target. When the German Luftwaffe retaliates, at least 80 American planes and 800 crew members are shot down.

Learning to fly a challenging plane did not deter Wolfe. As a boy on his family's farm at Aberdeen, S. Dakota in 1935, he had spotted an Army surveillance balloon. Thus began a lifelong love with aviation.

After enlisting in the U.S. Army in 1939, Wolfe failed his eye exam. When the eye doctor told Wolfe to go home and rest his eyes in a dark room and try again the next day, Wolfe agreed to do so. Instead, he remained in the waiting room. Each time the exam door opened, he memorized the eye charts – all nine of them. The next day he passed the exam.

In October 1942 Wolfe graduated from flight school, having learned Morse code, weather and astral navigation. In May 1943, he was promoted to Second Lieutenant of the 391st Bomb Group.

In January 1944 Wolfe's crew of seven received sealed orders that could only be opened after they had left the base at Miami. "Our plane had torpedo racks so my crew thought we were headed to Japan," he said. Instead, the orders stated their destination as England.

When an inexperienced navigator caused Wolfe's plane to be lost over the ocean, Wolfe used radio beacons to find the way. Nazis intercepted and misdirected Wolfe's plane towards a German-held air base in Africa. When he landed, they would capture him and his crew.

Wolfe was aware of the deception and veered away from the Nazis, landing at an Allied base in Liberia. After re-fueling and enduring a sand storm in the Sahara Desert, Wolfe flew around Spain and France, finally landing in England.

The night before D-Day, Wolfe and other Allied troops made final preparations of their planes for the invasion, including painting black and white stripes on the underside of Allied planes to help identify them in battle.

During the invasion, Allied aircrews avoided 16-foot-high logs which the Germans placed in fields and meadows at Normandy. German General Erwin Rommel had ordered their design and usage to deter paratroopers. The poles, which numbered more than one million, earned the nickname 'Rommel's Asparagus'.

Rommel served as field marshal of Germany's military ('Wehrmacht'). Referred to as 'Desert Fox' because of his excellent leadership of German forces in the battles of North Africa, Rommel knew air power could tie his tanks down during battles.

Crossed rifles placed by comrades honor a fallen soldier at Normandy. Poles on the beach are set by German General Rommel to deter advancement of troops.

He believed a tight defense was needed, should the beaches of Normandy be the point of an Allied invasion.

Rommel was right to be worried about American aircraft. On June 6, a myriad of planes took part in securing the beaches. As B-26 crews dropped bombs, P-47s and P-51s seized beach exits. Cargo planes carried wounded soldiers to safety and paratroopers dropped behind beaches and into villages to disrupt enemy defenses. Due to the high number of Allied missions that had destroyed German planes and bases before June 6, opposition in the air by German planes was minimal with only a handful taking part.

As with most battles that take place in the air, the success of D-Day by aircrews depended heavily on the teams of dedicated aircraft mechanics who ensured their safe flights.

Harrison Hull (second from left) stands with his aircraft mechanic crew at an airbase in England.

Shortly after midnight on June 6, Harrison 'Harry' Hull and other aircraft mechanics were awakened from their bunks at an airbase at Peterborough, England. "We were told to eat breakfast and get the planes ready to fly," said Hull. "The pilots would take off before dawn."

Hull served as crew chief of the 61st Squadron for the Eighth Air Force's 56th Fighter Group. Born in 1920 on a farm in

DeKalb County in Ind., Hull knew from an early age that he loved planes. "I told people I wanted to be an airplane driver," he said. "I didn't know the word for pilot."

After graduating from Athens High School in Tennessee in 1938, Hull enlisted in the Army Air Corps.

He was at Keesler Field in Biloxi, Mississippi, on December 7, 1941, when news arrived about the Japanese bombing of Pearl Harbor.

Hull trained as a plane mechanic, then was sent to work on P-47s at air bases at Peterborough, Colchester and Boxsted in England. Hull's eye for detail was quickly noticed and he was promoted to crew chief. "Our crews' missions were to bomb factories and strafe airports, cities, buildings," he said. "I made sure the planes were in working order."

Hull takes a break on the wing of a plane he helps to maintain as crew chief.

To deflect the stress of their work, crews assigned humorous names to planes. Hull's were named for Snow White's seven dwarfs. "One pilot wanted to be a doctor so we named his plane Doc," he said.

Camaraderie developed between flight mechanics and flight crews. At the end of each day, mechanics crews scanned the sky, praying each plane that left that morning would return. When they didn't, Hull found it difficult to handle. "I felt like President Lincoln when he lost an election," said Hull. "He said it was like stubbing your toe, but you're too big to cry."

CHAPTER 8

James Fall - Prisoner of War

During the months leading up to D-Day, Lt. James Fall of Marion, Ind., was assigned to the 391st Fighter Squadron of 366th Fighter Group, 9th Air Force. He flew combat missions in a P-47 Thunderbolt. This fighter was equipped with eight 50-caliber machine guns, bombs and rockets. "My mission was to destroy railroads, bridges, and German military supply depots," he said.

Even though Fall's plane was often shot at by the enemy, Fall never believed he was in danger. "I had seen buddies go down but didn't think it could happen to me," he said.

That belief changed at D-Day.

In March 1944 James Fall's pilot training is over. At 20 years old, he spends time in New York City awaiting combat deployment. In just three months he will be shot down and taken prisoner by German troops.

Fall flew against the enemy on June 6 and for several days afterward. On D-Day+4 (June 10), he was on his 21st combat mission over France when his plane suddenly lurched to the right. Glancing through the window, Fall was horrified to see a large, jagged hole in his plane's left wing. Flames of fire trailed from behind.

Swallowing the fear that threatened to choke him, Fall quickly donned his parachute and bailed out of his burning aircraft. He landed hard on his left leg and suspected he had broken it.

Looking up, Fall's heart sank as several male youth stood before him, guns cocked in his direction. He learned later they were members of the 12th Hitlerjugend Panzer

Division. Fall surrendered to the teens who marched him on his damaged leg to Dulag Luft, the German Air Force's interrogation center.

For seven days Fall was held in solitary confinement with little food or water. When German officials from the Luftwaffe rigorously interrogated him, demanding information about the American Army Air Corps, Fall refused to give more than his name, rank and serial number. His left leg ached, but no medical treatment was offered.

In July Fall and other American prisoners of war (POWs) were transferred to Stalag Luft III near Sagan, Poland. Fall's broken leg received medical attention by another POW who issued a request for materials to make a cast. Amazingly, the request was granted. With no other medical attention, Fall's leg healed properly.

Photo taken by German captors one month after Fall is shot down over Normandy reflects his lack of nutrition and well-being. His body weight drops by 80 pounds during his 10-month imprisonment.

Food served to the prisoners consisted mostly of cabbage soup and moldy bread. Over the next several months, Fall's body weight dropped by 80 pounds.

In January 1945 the POWs were marched 65 miles in blizzard conditions to Spremberg, Germany where they rode in boxcars to Stalag VII A near Moosberg.

On April 29, 1945, the 14th Armored Division of General Patton's Third Army liberated the camp at Moosberg. Ten months after his plane was shot down, Lt. James Fall was again a free man. "If it were not for food parcels and medical supplies from the American Red Cross and prayers from family and friends, I would not have survived," he said.

CHAPTER 9

Treating the Injured

Leo Scheer

The explosion ripping through the air almost knocked naval corpsman Leo Scheer off his feet. Standing at the stern (back) end of the vessel that approached Omaha Beach loaded with troops, he was horrified to view empty space where the bow (front) had been moments earlier. None of the dozens of sailors that had stood there remained. The boat had hit two mines hidden by the Germans in the English Channel's murky depths.

As enemy shells spattered the deck of what remained of Scheer's vessel, he obeyed orders to abandon ship. Scheer's body shivered as it sank into the frigid, churning waves. His pack of supplies threatened to pull him under.

By some miracle, Scheer made it safely to the Normandy shore. He averted his eyes from the drowned and rifle-ridden bodies around him. It was too late to offer medical help to those troops. Scheer hoped his skills as a medic would be of use to others.

Medics apply aid to an injured soldier.

Scheer had enlisted in the U.S. Navy in June 1942 after graduating from Huntington Catholic High School in Indiana. Following completion of boot camp at Great Lakes Naval Training Center in Illinois, Scheer was assigned to a hospital corps school.

Wearing a Red Cross arm band and helmet to identify him as a medic, Scheer searched the bodies of dead soldiers on the beach for medical supplies. "It was all I had to treat the wounded," he said. Bandages packaged in waterproof tins and packages of morphine would be of use to wounded soldiers.

Scheer lay nearly prostrate on the beach administering medical help. "Shells came in close," he said. "Even getting on your knees was risky." Morphine was a popular medicinal aid used to prevent shock from injuries and Scheer used it often. The use of dried plasma by combat medics was another medical innovation introduced during the war.

Allied troops learned to be alert for more than enemy fire. On one occasion American naval destroyers tried to silence a pillbox where the enemy was firing an 88-millimeter cannon. "The Germans behind that fortification had sunk ten of our boats," he said. "Our Navy was interested in taking it out."

But as the Navy fired on the pillbox, debris fell on Scheer and other Allied troops, causing fatalities. "We were being attacked by both sides," he said. Finally, an Allied battleship fired its guns at the pillbox, disabling it. Shelling on the ground troops ceased.

Day and night the clash to claim ownership of the Normandy beachheads continued, each side aiming lethal salvos at its enemy. Scheer rested for short bits of time when and where he could. "I buried myself under the sand and when I awoke, I crawled out, glad to still be alive," he said.

Upon discovering a trio of soldiers lying on the ground, Scheer was sad to discover two were dead. The third laying on his side was still breathing. An exam by Scheer revealed a bullet lay in the hip socket, narrowly missing a bone.

Scheer worked on the soldier for three days, checking on him often while caring for other wounded soldiers. By the third day, the soldier could be moved to a landing craft. From there he would be taken to a hospital ship and probably shipped back to England to a hospital. "I slept good knowing that guy had been helped," said Scheer.

As Robert 'Bob' Batchelder of Fort Wayne crawled down the side of his landing craft to a Higgins boat at Omaha Beach, his heavy bag of medical supplies strapped to his back nearly pulled him off balance. Of equal menace were the turbulent waves threatening to pull soldiers under as they dropped into the water. "Thankfully, I knew how to swim," said Batchelder.

Batchelder was a member of the 457th Medical Collecting Company, which supported the 82nd Airborne Division. The 457th retrieved injured and dead bodies on the battlefield.

After traversing the beach area amid gun fire, Batchelder helped pitch a 12-by-20-foot tent for a temporary field hospital. For five days he and other medical personnel treated casualties as best they could.

"We retrieved injured and dead bodies on the battlefield," said Batchelder. For five days he and other medical personnel treated casualties as best they could. "Morphine was a common pain reliever," he said. Penicillin would not be readily available until near the end of the war.

When Charles Valentine of North Manchester, Ind., arrived at Omaha with the 76th General Hospital a few days after June 6th, the carnage and smells threatened to overwhelm him. "Most of the dead bodies had been removed, but evidence of their recent presence remained," he said.

Born in Liberty Center, Ind., in 1924, Valentine was drafted into the U.S. Army in 1943. He received training as a medical technician at Camp Grant near Rockford, Ill. At

Vancouver, Canada, he learned skills needed for treating battle injuries in a hospital setting.

After sailing on a troop ship to England, Valentine helped establish hospitals along the southern coast near Southampton. "The hospitals were rumored to be used for an upcoming Allied invasion of Europe," he said. From Southampton Valentine prepared to sail with other medical personnel for France.

During the invasion, Valentine managed to block out the blood-bathed scenes around him to focus on treating the injured. Despite the passage of time, those scenes never left his mind. "Decades later, I can still hear sounds and smell odors that remind me of the invasion," he said.

CHAPTER 10

Eugene Cogan – Wounded Twice at Normandy

On June 6, 1944, Eugene Cogan of Avilla, Ind., prepared to lead troops of B Company, 115th Infantry Regiment, 29th Division down the gangplank onto Omaha Beach. His excellent marksmanship skills had caused Cogan to be chosen as first scout. He would be vulnerable to enemy fire from the Germans, but Cogan, 21, felt confident. "I was a good shooter and carried my 1903 Springfield scope rifle," he said. "I didn't think about dying."

As Cogan would find out, not everything in war goes as planned.

Cogan was born in 1922 in Kendallville, Ind. After graduating from Avilla High School in 1941, he worked at a machine shop in Mishawaka at 50 cents an hour before being drafted in February 1943 into the U.S. Army.

Cogan completed 11 weeks of basic training at Camp Wolters in Texas, before being assigned to B Company, 115th Infantry Regiment, 29th Division.

In spring 1944, he and 16,000 other troops boarded the prestigious Queen Elizabeth, converted to a troop ship, at New York City.

Gene Cogan's superior shooting skills earn him the position of first scout at Omaha Beach.

After landing at Plymouth, England, the troops completed 25-mile hikes and practiced landing on Britain's Slapton Sands. "The coast there was similar to France's," he said. Scuttlebutt said the training was for a European invasion, though soldiers were given no idea when or where it would take place.

They trained at night, using rope ladders to transfer from large ships to Higgins boats. "The only things that were different from rehearsal and the real thing," said Cogan, "is that we had no opposition and no live ammunition."

On June 5, the troops moved to Portsmouth where they were finally told their mission – they would hit France's Normandy beaches the next day.

Under enemy fire, Cogan and other Allied troops crossed the mine-ridden, quarter-mile stretch of beach filled with dead and wounded bodies. Later, he could not recall making it across the beach to the bluff where the Germans fired.

After securing the coast, the Allies began slowing moving inland. While patrolling through an orchard on a steep bluff in the Normandy region, Cogan was shot in the back. He fell and lay unconscious for several hours. When he awoke, he sadly viewed the bodies of fallen comrades around him.

When Cogan tried crawling in the direction of an aid station, a second sniper shot hit him in the leg. Cogan rolled down a hill and lay still. Upon awakening, he was startled to see faces peering down at him. Then he relaxed. They were men from his unit. "They had returned to retrieve dog tags from dead soldiers," he said.

Cogan was placed on a stretcher on the hood of a jeep and taken to a field hospital. Luckily, the bullet to his back only grazed him, but his left leg was broken. He was flown to an Allied hospital near Liverpool, England to receive more care and rehabilitation.

Cogan returned to the U.S. where he spent several months at a hospital at Fort Benjamin Harrison in Indianapolis. He was awarded a Purple Heart for sustaining injuries during combat.

Years later, Private First Class Cogan wrote a poem about his experiences at D-Day.

"I stood among the crosses of my buddies from Company "B", their crosses glistened in the Normandie sun – what a beautiful sight to see.

For just a moment my buddies were standing each by his cross, in battle dress, silently they pass in review – I saluted them as they returned to rest.

Three score years have passed since we landed in Normandie, many times I have wondered - why did they – and not me.

I have no answer to the question – but a little bit of me rests with my buddies in a place in Normandie."

CHAPTER 11

After D-Day

The weeks following D-Day continued to be challenging as the Allies fought through Nazi defenses. By August 1944, the Allies had pushed east across war-ravaged France and freed much of the country, including Paris.

Marching through Paris when the city was liberated impressed Richard Willey. "The Parisians lined the streets and threw flowers," he said. "They were so glad to see us." By the time the war ended in Europe in May 1945, Willey had collected souvenirs from his time as a soldier: Hitler youth T-shirt, silver Nazi dress bayonet, black bayonet, Nazi arm band, parachute, and a Luftwaffe (German Air Force) cap.

"Some parts of the military were quite an ordeal," Willey said, "but I'm proud to have been involved."

Six months after D-Day, Bob Batchelder served as a medic in the Battle of the Bulge.

After the war, he worked in the wholesale candy business. He and his wife Edna were parents to one son.

In May 1945, Don LeMaster helped to liberate the death camp located near Dachau, Germany. After the war, he returned to work at General Electric in Fort Wayne where he met his wife, Betty.

They became parents to two sons. In 1985 Don and Betty  returned to Europe. When residents of France discovered Don had fought for them in World War II, they thanked him.

Al Edwards' Seabees battalion later served in the South Pacific, making it the only Seabees battalion to serve in both European and Pacific Theaters. Edwards attended many military reunions and had the privilege of placing a wreath at the Tomb of the Unknown Soldier at Arlington Cemetery.

Gene Valentine saw the other side of medical care during the war when his appendix burst. "I was lucky to have experienced doctors take care of me," he said. "We all learned we could do things we didn't think possible during the war."

Leo Scheer was transferred to New Guinea to work in a hospital ward of soldiers suffering from shell-shock. At home, he became a charter member of the National World War II Museum in New Orleans.

George Banky re-enlisted at the end of the war. He traveled the world with the Navy during the 1950s and 1960s, living two years in Morocco.

Donald Lee, attached to Patton's 3rd Army, fought in the Battle of the Bulge. By the end of the war, he like other soldiers could not wait to get home. "When the troops on our ship saw the Statue of Liberty in New York City, we started cheering," he said. "It was great!"

In 2013 Gene Cogan accepted an invitation to represent the 29th Division at a D-Day celebration in the French village of Carentan. His name was added to a plaque unveiled in

remembrance of the invasion and on a section of road in the village. "I'm a better person for having served during World War II," he said.

Gene Dettmer received five battle stars for his involvement in the war, including Utah Beach. In 1970 Dettmer completed his high school education through a GED. Although he didn't receive a diploma from Ossian High School, Dettmer was included as an honorary member of the class of 1944.

After his discharge from military service, Dean Reckard owned and operated a truck repair business in Huntington. "I was honored to serve in World War II," he said. A son served in the Army.

One of Charles Dunwoody's proudest moments as a soldier occurred at the end of the war when he and other chaplains carried freed Allied POWs to the American lines. "We had 10 to 12 men to a jeep," he said. At home in Ohio, Dunwoody farmed, married, and served his church as a minister.

Bob Staggs was in Czechoslovakia when the war ended. Upon being discharged in December 1945, he returned to Muncie where he drove a truck for the Coca-Cola Company. He married and became a parent to two sons. "I'd do my military service again, but I'm glad we kept it off of our soil," he said.

In spring 1945, the Americans met the Russian military at the Elbe River in Germany. "We let the Russians take over Berlin," said Ray Willig. He continued to serve in the military during the Korean War and beyond for 27 years, retiring at the rank of Master Sergeant.

For his efforts as an exemplary crew chief Staff Sergeant Hull was awarded a Bronze Star for heroic meritorious achievement. He worked as a plane mechanic at Smith Field in Fort Wayne and for Bunge in Decatur, while earning commercial, instrument, and multi-engine pilot ratings. Hull's two sons served in the military.

On Don Wolfe's 52nd mission during the war, his right engine was hit by a German fighter. He managed to stay in the air long enough to bomb a German headquarters before arriving safely back to his base. For his heroic maneuvers Wolfe received the Distinguished Flying Cross. He retired from the Air Force in 1964 with a flight log of 4,720 hours.

After Jim Fall's release from the German prison, he returned to his unit to fly through the end of the war. Later, he earned a dentistry degree from Indiana University and worked at that career in Marion, Ind.

He and Ethel Mae married and became parents to three children. "I do not regret my time as a prisoner of war," said Fall. "I'm proud of my service because I wanted to do my part for our country." Photo below is of a P-47 Thunderbolt like Fall flew.

CHAPTER 12

More Facts about D-Day

The Normandy invasion incorporated 156,000 troops, 5,300 ships and 11,000 planes on five major beachheads. More than 50,000 British troops hit Gold and Sword beaches, while 9,000 British troops landed with the Canadians at Juno Beach, encountering heavy opposition. While far from easy especially during the first few tough hours, the landings at Gold and Sword proceeded in generally orderly fashion.

While achieving the initial objective at D-Day of overtaking the beaches, the cost of the Allied victory was high. According to research done by the U.S. National D-Day Memorial Foundation, Allied personnel killed during the initial D-Day invasion numbered approximately 4,414.

By early July, as the fighting continued further inland, the Allies had sustained 8,975 deaths with many more troops injured.

This monument stands above Omaha Beach in memory of the men who died to free this part of Europe.

It reads: "The Allied forces landing on this shore which they call Omaha Beach liberate Europe June 6th, 1944."

On June 8, 1944, the U.S. First Army began using 170 acres just beyond the beaches at Normandy in the Colleville-sur-Mer area to bury soldiers. This temporary site was the first American cemetery on European soil in World War II.

Today the Normandy American Cemetery and Memorial in Colleville-sur-Mer contains 9,388 white crosses marking the locations of men and women who lost their lives in the D-Day landings and ensuing operations.

In 2007, a $30 million Normandy Visitors Center opened at the cemetery. Parts of the cemetery were filmed in the Hollywood movie *Saving Private Ryan*.

The Author's Reflections of D-Day and Normandy:

In 2017 my husband and I participated in a 10-day World War II group tour of Europe. We traveled 2,000 miles via motor coach, visited many sites in Belgium, Germany, France, and Luxembourg.

Throughout the trip, we fluctuated between feelings of exhilaration and sadness at being in many of the same places that American soldiers had been -- a foxhole used during the Battle of the Bulge, Paris' Notre Dame, Hitler's Eagle's Nest in Berchtesgaden, Patton's grave, courtroom in Nuremberg used during the war trials of Nazi criminals for crimes against humanity, and more.

My favorite part of the trip was standing on Omaha Beach on June 6. Standing at the water's edge, I looked back at the quarter mile stretch of beach that extended to the bluffs where German soldiers and guns had been stationed. It was moving to think of the thousands of young boys (I call them that as many had quit school at age 17 to enlist) who had landed there.

What terror they must have experienced, drawing near to the French coast. My hands would have been frozen to the sides of the Higgins boat and I doubt if I could have run off the ramp on legs like jelly.

One question I always ask a veteran who has seen combat: How did you face that experience? Weren't you scared?

They always answer one of two ways: "Of course, we were scared. Anyone who tells you they weren't is lying."
OR
"We were too young and dumb to be scared. Our training taught us to face the enemy."

When I give talks about D-Day, I share these honest confessions. Keep in mind, these were young men, many of whom were farm boys who had never traveled outside of their own state. They had been forced to leave home, become soldiers and then be shipped an ocean away from friends and family. They had spent months learning how to perform courageous acts in battle to help people they would never meet regain their freedom.

In letters to friends and family written the night before the invasion they could not mention that within hours they would face death. It must have been a challenge to appear calm with their thoughts, though surely their hands were shaky with trepidation. Maybe it was put down to the rocking of waves in the ships.

I'm amazed that anyone survived the war. I'm equally amazed that anyone came home in their right minds. But they did. They got jobs, went to college, married, raised families and attended church. Many were leaders in their communities, volunteering to help where needed and donating to worthy causes. Many never spoke about their times of military service during World War II. The attributes of courage and dedication went largely unnoticed.

I'm thankful for modern medicine that has extended the lives of these veterans, allowing me to interview 250+, some of whom were 100 years old.

All military veterans are deserving of respect, but especially those in this group. They set the stage for military service. They were not perfect – no one is – but in my book they were pretty close.

World War II Timeline

1933

Adolph Hitler is appointed chancellor of Germany; the first of dozens of concentration camps over Europe is established at the German village of Dachau.

1938

Germany invades Austria; Hitler holds his last annual rally in Nuremberg, which draws one million people who support his practices and ideals.

1939

Hitler invades Poland and Czechoslovakia, causing both countries to surrender; Nazis begin persecuting Polish Jews; the United States begins selling military supplies to British and France to support their efforts to oppose the Nazis; Great Britain, Australia, New Zealand, Canada, South Africa and India declare war on Germany- this is the official start to World War II.

1940

Germany invades Denmark, Norway, Belgium, Netherlands, Luxembourg, and France and all surrender; Winston Churchill becomes Britain's new Prime Minister; Italy joins the war with Germany; the Battle of Britain begins when Germany bombs London and other British cities -- the 'Blitz' continues on London for 57 nights, killing more than 40,000 citizens – even though the bombing continues through much of 1941, Great Britain refuses to surrender and Hitler puts off an invasion; Japan joins Italy and Germany in fighting the Allies; American president Roosevelt is elected to a third term, the only time an American president will serve more than two; Roosevelt bans racial discrimination in war-industry employment.

1941

Germany invades Greece; the United States continues to send military equipment and other supplies to the Allies with payment deferred until after the war; Germany attacks the Soviet Union; the Soviet Union joins the Allies; Japan attacks Pearl Harbor, along with other Allied bases in the Pacific and Asia, the result being the United States and Great Britain declare war on Japan; Germany and Italy declare war on the United States.

1942

The Nazis establish a plan to kill European Jews via death camps; Japanese troops take control of large portions of East Asia and the Pacific, including Hong Kong, Singapore, the Philippines, Thailand, Malaysia and Burma; United States invades North Africa; United States wins the Battle of Midway, a major turning point in the war in the Pacific; people of Japanese heritage are interned in the United States.

1943

Italy is invaded by the Allies and surrenders; Mussolini is removed from power; Italy begins secret peace talks with the Allies and eventually declares war on Germany; Churchill, Roosevelt and Stalin meet to discuss Operation Overlord, the Allied invasion of Normandy, France, against Germany's armed forces.

1944

In January General Dwight D. Eisenhower takes charge of planning Operation Overlord, which takes place in June;

Allies push German forces towards Germany, liberating many cities including Paris; Roosevelt is elected to his fourth term as United States president; in December, the Germans attempt a last-ditch effort to overcome the Allies by splitting their troops, a strategy that becomes known as the Battle of the Bulge; Allied island-hopping in the Pacific liberates the Philippines.

1945

Prisoners at Dachau and dozens of other death camps placed throughout Europe are freed to the horror of Allied troops who witness their emaciated bodies; Allies defeat the Germans in the Battle of the Bulge; Allies take the Pacific island of Iwo Jima; Churchill, Roosevelt and Stalin meet for the last time in Yalta to discuss the end of the war and how to divide Germany; in April Roosevelt dies and Vice President Harry S. Truman is sworn in as president; Mussolini is captured and executed by his own people; Hitler commits suicide in his underground bunker in Berlin; Germany surrenders in May; Truman declares the end of the war on May 8 as V-E Day (Victory in Europe); United States drops atomic bombs on the Japanese cities of Hiroshima and Nagasaki; the Soviet Union declares war on Japan; Japan's Emperor Hirohito accepts the Allies' terms of surrender on August 14, which becomes known as V-J Day (Victory over Japan); American troops begin returning home, while others are assigned to Japan and Europe during the Allied period of occupation.

D-Day Glossary

artillery: Method of defense and offense used to support Allied landings at Normandy from warships.

Atlantic Wall: Germany's first line of defense in the West. It lay along France's coast and consisted of fortified gun emplacements, beach obstacles and mine fields.

casualty: Soldiers killed, injured, captured or missing in action after a battle.

D-Day: Military term signifying the date when an attack will be launched. By common usage it has come to stand for the 1944 invasion of Normandy but can refer to other events in history.

glider: Light, engineless airplanes designed to float after being towed aloft or launched from a catapult.

hedgerows: Fences made of dirt, trees, bushes and stone several feet high and several feet thick, making them nearly impenetrable for Allies in Normandy.

infantry: American divisions of 14,000 troops divided into regiments and battalions. They formed the backbone of attack and defense forces on D-Day.

Luftwaffe: Name of the German Air Force.

Overlord: Code name for the entire Allied campaign to invade and liberate France and Western Europe.

rations: Fixed portions of food or goods usually considered necessary for survival.

sabotage: Treacherous action, such as the destruction of property, to defeat or hinder a cause.

sortie: Flight of combat aircraft when on a military mission.

About the Author

Kayleen Reusser has interviewed hundreds of World War II veterans and published their stories in magazines, newspapers. Her books and other products are available on Amazon.

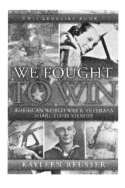  

Reusser and her husband participated in a 10-day World War II tour of Europe, visiting Normandy, Remagen Bridge, Paris, Nuremberg, Bastogne, Munich, Berchtesgaden, Pegasus Bridge and other sites.

Reusser presents talks about the trip and her veteran interviews to groups. Her books are available on Amazon. Discover more about Reusser's history-related writing projects through her free email newsletter at www.KayleenReusser.com.

During a WWII tour of Europe, Reusser and her husband stand in a foxhole in Belgium used during the Battle of the Bulge.

Index

Made in the USA
Monee, IL
13 January 2021